AF323916

THE BROKEN FACE OF SUMMER

THE BROKEN FACE OF SUMMER

Poems by

Michael Hogan

Duck Down
Fallon, NV
1981

Grateful acknowledgement is made to the editors of the following publications in which some of these poems first appeared: *The Paris Review, Poetry NOW, kayak, National Forum, The Westigan Review, Cedar Rock, The Greenfield Review, SCREE, Blue Moon, The Hollow Spring Review of Poetry, Magazine, Signatures, Moon Pony, and the New Monitor Anthology of Magazine Verse.*

Front cover design: Kirk Robertson

ISBN 0-916918-16-5

Library of Congress Catalog No.: 81-68829

Publication of this book has been assisted, in part, by receipt of a grant from the National Endowment for the Arts, a federal agency.

Typeset by Desert Graphics, Inc. Fallon, Nevada

A Windriver Book
Duck Down
PO Box 1047
Fallon, NV 89406

for Jojo

SOMEBODY'S MARY ANNE

Do you know what it is as you pass
to be loved by strangers?
                                        --Whitman

And the next day we left the chimera of Lordsburg
and headed north: Alamogordo, Corrizo, Gran Quivera,
the burlesque of Vegas, its town dump a monument
to Detroit insomniacs, its Main Street peopled by beings
pale enough to have been exposed to the light
by some dumb thunderclap of rage
turning over a rotting plank.

Then north again, headed for Durango
in the nameless, invisible doom of the southwestern night:
the rocks ghostly, the hills anesthetized with dust,
intolerant, omniverous
and the road (No Rest Area For The Next 70 Miles)
without purchase, a great slide into darkness,
against all returning.

It was Questa we stopped at.
Questa on the Red River. And you, lost child
of a lost city, somebody's Mary Anne,
after all the digested humiliations of old men
and improvised passions, picked up on 61 where
the road dips precipitously down some slashing of the hills.
You, sweet ember, smoke of honey,
cast up on the sandbar of interstates and Fina gas stations.

We had it there (didn't we?)
in cottage #13, cool after a shower taken together,
spilling the hot liquid of our dreams,
marbling our lives like lava in the hills,
or beef on packing trains headed north
and whistling us awake in the sheet-soaked dawn.

ERNEST HEMINGWAY - 1961

When the sun comes early
through eastern windows
and a single horsefly buzzsaws the air
it is then I rise from bed
my dreams of amputation, of teeth lost,
cloaked in the amnesia of another day
overwhelmed with trivia.

We make our own rules and lose by them.
This morning after a breakfast of coffee
and ice water I walk to the corner
feeling my liver dissolve in a
cacophony of stale beer and bad whiskey.
June drips a melody sweet as rose water
and the town wakes slowly.

These things are substance, Mary, not prelude.
Only what moves us has meaning.
The rest is lost in a weed-choked yard
or the gutter with brown cigarette butts,
orange peels, used condoms.
When words fail, the hammer drops.
Living can never be its own excuse.

I have carried this gun in dreams:
quiet ones in which a wounded animal
is given peace by the hunter's grace.
Now hunter and animal, I find myself
precipitating an act gentle as June rain.
And in this dazzling pellet-rain
I'll sing the best of all men's songs.

Take care, Mary, of the cats. Smile
at those who call me coward.
These last weeks so free of conflict

are quiet also of energy and force.
I am become abstract as a moveable feast,
my life arbitrary, capricious as a poem of Pound's.
Only the gun gives me substance
this trigger my clearest, most careful line.

THE BROKEN FACE OF SUMMER

The cicadas avalanched that summer
leaving each morning breathless
in the frosted glare of the day.
Demented doves surged in and out among the trees,
weaving a pattern tight and intricate
as Queen's Knight to King's Bishop Four
or the Gospel of St. John.
We slept naked in the copper glare
of Saturday's, stinking like trout
wrapped in newspapers left out in the sun.
We slept together but alone: priest and novice,
the candles of our dreams fluttering out,
your touch like the taste of Greek wine,
dry, heavy as rosin.
And nothing would come together:
not the soporific images of poems left unwritten
nor the few months of work to pull us
sleek and green to the cool September rains.

I wrote it down, Zelda:
how you danced pale and desperate
as a moth beneath the Chinese lanterns,
your mind delicate as Dresden,
your face brittle, always close to tears.
I wrote it down
not trusting to memory
the oppressive mercury of your moods
or Gerturde's somber explications.

The Filipino houseboy, do you remember?
And your dress at cocktails, cool as Margaritas,
torn, radiant with sleek Spanish vowels
when the last headlight winked down the gravel drive.

I wrote it down. I wrote it all down.
As if the discipline of words
could landscape the garden and the wide lawn beyond;
as if the words themselves could hold innocence
rushing out like a neap tide.

How will they remember us, Zelda?
How recall that summer?
Two porcelain figures on the marble stairs
waving *Goodbye! Goodbye!*
The smell of incense in L'eglise de St. Jerome.
Zelda, how will they think of us?
A wristlet of yellow flowers
discarded by an open window.
The crystal wineglass empty, the fine stem broken.
This last, a wedding gift, wasn't it,
from my mother or yours?

THE CONDOR

Dark and lugubrious, his eyes
signify no intent beyond brooding.
All day he has been poised on thermals
as if the land would rise like a hand
and say: *Blessings! Blessings!*
Observant as a child who watches
the sidewalk for a dollar
dropped by chance along the way to school.
He waits. The dollar's never there.
It is a story like the one they tell prisoners
of a world outside the wall to keep them
simple with hope.

Now he's passed the rift valley
empty of game and descends
smooth as a spent bullet to the Bay.
He feeds there on salmon spilled
by the fishing boats.
It is always less than he wanted.
He dreams of a freshly killed goat
on a grassy hill near Monterey,
a calf, a yearling torn by rocks
or the teeth of wild dogs.
But it is always something less.
Today salmon. Tomorrow a rabid skunk,
a coyote dropped by fever.

The Apache said the bird made thunder
by beating its wings. The Apache said
lightning was born in the condor's eyes.
I tell my son the old legends
but think instead of losses. Think of the doomed
Irish days of my grandfather and the miles
he drifted; his eyes red after a fifth of Jameson
as this great lost searcher's looking out at a world.

Always one which gave less than the dreams.
But he told me the legends. How there
was once a people whose poetry
thundered on Tara's hills, whose eyes flashed lightning,
when the world was young
and no man could measure the breadth of a life.

It was before the factories, before the wife
dead with the third child and the child stillborn.
It was before the friends imprisioned, the dole,
the immigration. *I sometimes think,* he said,
that life is fine unless you stay too long at it.

We call the condor an endangered species
and like the sound of that captured phrase.
And the condor, his wings transcendent
as an old memory beat: *Alexander! Alexander!*
With no other worlds to conquer.

TELEGRAM

During the War everyone on our street
was afraid of Western Union
how the Gold Star always followed.
We saw curtains drawn, venetian blinds
collapse in grief, the children stand
soberly as old men talking
"At the Bulge. A forest in Belgium.
So close to victory," the paper said.

When Sammy came home from Nam
he had an oil burner
five dime bags a day but he cleaned up
got a job driving for Holsum Bakery.
Then he quit to write his novel.

Sammy's mother told me
when I saw her in the local market
that I got better looking every day.
She said, "You're *such* a handsome boy!"
and hugged me.

So I didn't ask about the novel.
When someone is speaking to me of loss,
in the way they stand
is the sound of a doorbell ringing
in a corner house with green shingles
as all the neighbors watch
grateful it is not them.

TWO CHILDHOOD FRIENDS

I return home after sixteen years to discover that
they are both firemen. They will retire with good pensions
in a few years. They get to march in the St. Patrick's Day
parade. My mother watches them and taps her feet. They
have investments in real estate. They are comfortably
overweight. At the Hibernian Club we drink beer and
shots, and remember how dangerous we were as kids, how
we terrorized the neighborhood. Our impact was lasting.
The wooden benches at the park still bear the scars of our
immortality.

Two men in firemen's suits who get to chop down doors
with double-headed axes, who get to wear outrageous
hats, speed through the neighborhood, clomp around in
big boots.

Sixteen years and nothing has changed. They tell me
I should stay, give up teaching, join the Department. I do
not even tell my wife. The idea is so absurd. But at night,
when I hear sirens my hands reach for a polished brass
pole, my feet stretch towards asbestos boots.

IN THE SAME PLACE

He was deaf as a drainpipe
in a Midwestern drought,
had roommates in college who made love to girls
with him in the same room,
and when Professor Tannin turned--
red bowtie to the board--
he missed half the day's notes.

His vocal cords were strung with helium,
the voice high, feminine, absurd.
And, though never really cruel,
we knew he was not real in our world.

But like a spy he listened
with his eyes to what our lips said,
chose friends from those which moved: Kindness.
He even learned the odor of woman
balanced between two moons.

These days the delicate machinery
of talk is splintered with sunlight.
And balanced in the same place
I climb the stairway of her lips
bewildered and joyful when they move: Love.

CRITIQUE OF NEW FICTION

Words have to point beyond themselves
which is not to say *answer questions.*
But when a significant thing happens--
a woman running down the street
her heel broken, her dress in disarray--
we must be given the weather that day
the sound her breath makes torn and frightened.

Or say it's October and the moon unfurls
like a Moslem battle flag.
We must be carried beyond ourselves,
the image on the telescopic plate which says
another place for us to walk on
and speak instead of
a white house anchored beneath it
like a racing yacht in Newport harbor.

The world is spinning like a child's toy,
the sun is strangling with pyrotechnics,
the whole galaxy is flying outward
and nothing holds, not really, not for one breath
except words which say: *here!*
and certain lives which echo.

BARTLEBY THE SCRIVNER

--The Tombs, 1853

At first I was an excellent copyist
working by vaguest of candlelights
eyes like dead moons
body cramped, worm upon a hook.
a useful man.

Untrustworthy as she was beautiful, my wife
had men into the flat those days.
A head clerk was one:
his face like those you see
upon dusty canvases in attics,
gold chain against prodigious vest.
It was then began, I suppose,
this mania for self-destruction.
I refused, simply, to work
though I came punctually to my stool,
copying pad and pen before me.

Love consists wholly of paradoxes:
she, warm as a summer equinox;
myself, a profile of fog and rainy days
crushed into weariness as day
inexorably followed tedious day.
And day beyond day I sat upon my stool
speaking to none beyond the lawyer
who employed me, and only then
to refuse gloomily and with feigned regret
any task he assigned.
My wife prospered with lovers.
I pawned a necklace the lawyer gave her
and for several days drowned in pewter pots.
Occasionally, I discovered small sums
pinned to the inside of her petticoats
and these, too, converted to drink.

Finally it came. The reckoning.
Would it please you to quit me, sir?
            It would not.
Then, trespasser and vagrant, I was
arrested, taken to the Halls of Justice.
Victim, who refused to be one.
Should I have worked, then? Copying?
Should I have killed her?
And is this place any worse
than the one left by my refusals?

To have written so much and said nothing
beyond this mania for self-justification.
My wife, I've heard, lives an erratic
unpunctual life, has many lovers.
This seems no point in pursuing this.
We live by our wounds.

AGENDA

Red ginger tea with honey against the cold.
Yet some days nothing works:
the dogs restless, that cat lost somewhere
in the year's first snow.
We continue but the wrong words
choose us even before we say them.

Life becomes a procession
of more or less lonely people
and one is so many of them
who can be sure if the one beside us at the bar
truly is a separate person.

Letters like poems never written
chant their accusations.
But it is not indifference
rather absence of miracle
a city which has closed all its windows.
This dismal morning it opens one
slowly looks out on the icy street
watches people hurrying to work
discovers there is no gift
beyond the sinuous search for engagement.

Angel of depression, today we will
not run from you.
Angel of boredom, we refuse to believe
you exist.
Demon of emptiness, possess us
that we might find the words: snow on aspens
ice on Clear Creek, birds at the feeder.
That we may exorcise you: cinnamon sugar
on homemade bread, the cat returned
from the storm,
the storm itself raging against our flickering light.

UNCHARTED

Light years away the future hangs
opaque and luminous as the Clouds of Magellan.
We are spinning out of this world like silkworms
and you tell me: no one asks
the important questions anymore except
college sophomores or professors of philosophy
like old ladies fingering rosaries,
finding the answers marked clearly
as Sirius, Belatrix, the Orian Nebula
on a winter skychart.

We are drinking beer together
after fifteen years of turnings, doubling back.
And you say: one night in Mexico everything
was clear, so clear, for one astounding instant.
But there was no one to tell
and the girl did not speak Enlish.
And you've never been surprised again.

PRAYER

Things change. Now she is my woman.
A honeysuckle wind dusts the flagstone walk
with pollen. The desparate monotony of winter
gone at her touch.
And I wear a green jacket
speak of a second child.

Once in a prison chapel after father's death
I spent the entire morning trying to pray
but grief had undone even that trembling
stick of faith, my life frayed into darkness.
I trusted no one, least of all the cosmos
its vacuum of meaning collapsing into the void.

This morning, her touch is benediction.
Her eyes absolve me surer than Malchiasidech.
There is still snow, heavy in the mountains.
There is also a letter from home reminding me
he's been gone four years this April.
But I hold her closer
and slowly my lips begin to move.

MOSES

On that day, liaison and ringmaster,
he was shaman of a tribe which listened
to no Earth-bound voice, found no miracle in Sun
who scorched their wasted land
or Moon whose pale light wakened wolves
to find their naked flock
on some bloodied hill.

In that burning world, Egypt's briered
backyard, what wonder bushes burned
and that a voice spoke, heard once--never again.
In that hard world, Egypt's wretched
rock quarry, tablets made of stone told
a story, once heard, a nation the same--never again.

His genius--which could not let his people be--
at the lodges of the Seneca, the camps of the Dakota
would make warriors smile.
They'd have kept him, fed him in charity
and women grinding corn
send him to the brook for water
or in spring to fields
where he would gather berries.

His genius could not let those people in.
His people born far from fields of corn,
plains dark with buffalo
were chosen for some high motive:
sufferers, moaners, survivors of disaster,
to joy in what divides them from the world.
This joy, this gift, legacy of him
who spoke to Yahweh, the Inscrutable,
whose Voice--once heard--never again.

Now only the sweet conversation of Sun,

gentle song of Moon quietly sensual
and the brooding growl of Thunder
muttering his way across the sky.

RETAINING WALL

It is still June, two weeks before solstice,
but deep, deep into summer this side of the Gila.
Palo verde blossoms are crisp as corn fritters
and the Pantano Wash hard as stucco,
cracked like a windshield struck by a rock.
The sun, uncompromising and vigorous,
blitzkriegs the earth, the rye grass,
the bare shoulders of my son
digging a ditch for the retaining wall.

Beyond the house where the land
slopes towards the wash, we plan the walls.
One will hold the beams to brace the porch;
the other the earth, the run of the wash
in flood season. He sees this with a man's eye:
the clear belief in possibilities which comes
from knowing a deep wound heal, feeling a bone knit,
finding at last a father there when the blood blisters,
the gnats hang heavy as clouds,
the old bad dreams return
or new ones come.
Finding a father at last.

This whole business of building,
what a fine thing! I tell him.
The crossbeams exactly thirty-four and a half inches down
and notched
and fitting snug as any knife in its sheath
or as she and I in the old days fit
before other walls no men remember building
in places one cannot forget.
And I am thinking: these whole days together,
rich as strawberry creamcakes
we make in the evening, fresh and cool,
and the strawberries fat as the Hope Diamond
and sweet.

The sun is relentless, the days long,
the work hard. Each day a new ache,
a muscle one had forgotten, a joint
creaking in its socket like an old watch.

But each moring we rise together new,
father and son, as if we were the first.
And in the evening, the work done,
we sit together in the quiet yard
and watch the day falling like a shooting star.

FOR A CHILD IN MERINO, AGE 8

The water in the intake ditch
is too cold and muddy.
No one would go there to play.
But two boys did one late afternoon
after birthday cake and Kool-Aid.
All along the reservoir that next day
men searched and could not find
the children slipping deeper into the silt
the delicate web of their muscles too soft
their breath not desperate enough
against the cold hand
of the South Platte's April overflow.

This morning it surrendered one of them
the body too bloated to be of use.
More money for the mortician
the flower shop downtown.
More news for the bored folks
at taverns to chew on.
Such a cold and muddy reason to be born.

The ditch should have held on
to what it took so easily
should have let him sleep among
the night crawlers and crawdaddies
on a soft bed of irrigation silt.
Instead he'll be drained of all that's human
filled with formaldehyde, deodorized
dressed like a tiny doll
.placed in a coffin with a silken headrest.

One day the silk will begin to rot
the coffin's seams will weaken.
One day the summer rains will bear him back
return him to the silt

from which we rescued him too late.
But now he lies in a polished box
to be carried to a grieving church
to be driven in a limousine
out to a grassy hill.

Child of muddy waters in the late afternoon
lost lily in a forgotten pond
forgive us this civilized outrage
forgive us this last and useless journey
before you quietly come to rest.

HOW A PLANET STAYS IN ORBIT

All morning the cottonwood
has been speaking. It began
when the house was barely awake,
not semaphore but a voice clearly distinguishable
which sang from all the nerve endings
which tumbled down the taproots,
which made the earth tremble
deep inside itself.

On a clear day you can see
forty miles to the Santa Ritas.
The tourists are amazed.
But where they come from,
Venus, millions of miles away,
clear as a barrel cactus,
is pointing south.

Here is the cottonwood
banal as a course in Contemporary Lit
until one day when you could have been
anyplace else but were not
some poem sings from everywhere inside you.
Then the earth trembles.
It spins far out, twinkling toward Venus
like a northern star.

And this is what the cottonwood is saying.
A difficult line if we are
not quiet enough, amazed enough.
It sings:
    This Earth is sweet as cherry brandy.
It rubs the warm Earth's belly.
And the planet spins in ecstasy,
it rushes out into space again and again
and then returns
hungry for our quiet songs.

FIRST ANNIVERSARY

People write to ask if we are well:
our car abandoned in the street
snow billowing in the hallway
and the wind sweeping tiredly
with her cold broom.
If things were better we could not bear it
unaccustomed as we are to success,
the well-dressed stranger passing by
but never stopping.

This worst winter in sixty years
brutalizes even the sky: a sun
dirty as waste cotton, trees
rattling their ivory limbs.
Somewhere further south are white doves
decorating the sky like Japanese kites;
girls in pastel halters
dance the afternoon on open patios,
and only the dead know or the very old
it is the same sky, the same sun.

CONVERSATION WITH A HOUSEWIFE

once you are here
there are many places you can never go
                    --Richard Shelton

Say even now you can't decide.
And this not Tinker Creek or Sabino Canyon
but coffee at six, last year's flies dead
between the screen and the window you slide back for air.
It's no longer there: long mornings in bed,
color patches on the gray cotton quilt.

There is a new priest, Mother says,
at Our Lady of Good Hope.
And out on I-10 just before the highway
breaks for Nogales your child saw
a sea of yellow flowers, Mama, wave after
wave all the way to the hills.

The cottage is milk-sweet and warm in the sun.
And you read somewhere meteorites arc to the earth
invisibly all day; whole generations of insects
appear each March invisibly beneath the elms.
But the afternoon becomes a carnival of bruises
and later, naked in the bathroom, brushing your teeth
over and over, you tell yourself: *Never again,* but
the shredded card from the escort service
clings to the side of the bowl. If only one were whole
or even seven again with father (*Oh, Father*) tossing
coins in the shadows of deep pools.

Parents are so briefly father and mother
and briefer friends. One returns at Christmas
to find them children; or one dead, the other
mailing holy cards to Robert and Amy, pulling them back
by guilt for their lost faith.
Grandmother, you tell them, *is very holy.*
But then, they ask, *why mean?*
Then you explain as one explains the cruelty
of one child to another. Grandmother.

If only one had something to sell, family jewels,
a good diamond. To be assured of value
even for what one owns. Or if one could touch again
that ineffable grace which pulls us from ourselves.
Or if there were something beyond memory,
that catalogue of losses, history without revelation.
Your honeymoon at Lake Desolation, the Adirondacks
quietly deep, the village asleep, that cabin
half-hidden in marsh grass, the touch of his skin,
the rush of wild geese at dawn. To be young is to think
those days could make these easier.

So you discover there is no question to decide.
What it means is what it means:
Something. Nothing. And not the place
but maybe always a place, what you were there
and what's become of you as the flowers
drop petal by petal into a stream forever flowing
and them irrecoverable forever.

But still, meteorites do arc to earth invisibly
even now. Whole generations of insects organize
their hierarchies beneath the elms. These things
go on even now as he comes up the flagstone walk.
He will ask how your day was
wondering why you cry so easily.
And even now as your man
arcs his back with a question that is his life,
even now you have nothing to say.

WARRIORS

Because the Chiricahuas formed a haven
in a sea of arid grassland, volcanic ash,
because the manzanita and sycamore
gave cover along the whole north face,
because there was finally no place left
over the whole earth.

But always when the question is asked
about your life
the answer you give depends only
upon who does the asking.

Cochise said, *Because there is nothing left
but blood.*

He plundered their horses, cattle.
He stole their grain.
Angry with losses he brought his people
down from the grassy knoll of Sugarloaf Mountain
to speak the price of this breathing land.
He could not know these Irish peasants
driven by the sea into his lances,
or by the English feared more than him,
the famine, crippling days on packed boats,
holds of Atlantic steamers.

He saw only the full heat of the desert
and their white skin,
shaded canyon bottoms, streams fed by snows
from the north,
their gleaming rifles knowing
worse places to die.

The Irish officer leading a troop
of cavalry along the weathered rock face,

past the boulders balanced like throwing knives
or a warrior's lance, knew blood
speaking to blood.
In his journal we find:
Capital runs out like a squeezed sponge.
Old men speak of what they have to lose.
Young men of taking.

BALTIMORE CATECHISM, VOLUME II

All morning I have been trying to find a way
to be alive in the world,
telling myself: it's the holidays, the place:
dessicated rye grass in front, the back littered
with broken things: bricks, planks, crockery.
This morning under December bells
in the random and tentative sun
scrubbed children race from Mass at St. Augustin's
home to sausages and sweet rolls, with unleavened
Eucharist pure as breast milk on their tongues.
I have neither slept nor eaten. In the cold drizzle
of the side yard I smoke my last cigarette:
solitary, inflexible, griefless; making ceremony
of each inhalation, repudiating faith and hope
as cattle on the Navajo reservation again this year
numbed by cold and poor feed
began melting into the earth days before they fell.

I remember once in North Carolina
at the arch of a drawbridge
there was a Black man hanged for
some nameless truth
from a six-by-eight supporting a Pepsi sign.
I raced by there telling myself:
It has nothing to do with you, go on, go on.
Beyond the bridge was the low smoke of the city
then a wharf, a launch slowing in and
a quiet crowd of people watching with that same
forlorn passivity the cows had.
I had a pistol then, heavy caliber shells,
and knew in one flashing moment I could wake
that crowd like Christ in the temple.
But across the road were pear trees in full
and frosty bloom, the twigs and branches
standing up from limbs like the hair

of a drowned woman on the floor
of a windless, tideless sea.
And they saw nothing. Nothing.

How could I remain there, that niggard life,
the wood-burn, the coal-burn, the squat shapes
of rusted Chevys littering the road East?
And the table where Justice sat was piled high
with sophistry and hundred dollar bills.
West, in the Arizona sun I crashed
through the underbrush, and fell
lighting my last candle to the angel of meaning.
Then I awoke in that red haze
feeling no blow, tasting no blood, but down
anyway for the count. I stayed down
convicted of everything but complicity
in the shabby creed of the hangman.

One morning, after the absolutions
and indulgences of years, I saw Justice:
a pitiful schizoid woman, leering,
hawking remorse, conformity like
Good Humor bars on a summer afternoon.
So I put on the rusted armor
of my father's good name and walked
out into the sun: a child, no gun this time
only scars tough as chainmail but Achillian,
vulnerable as a turtle's egg to cormorants.
I went down from the walled and ruined hill
toward the city and the birds
drew nearer and nearer, the liquid silver
of their voices unceasing, urgent.

The slow constellations wheel on.
It is dawn, then sunset for a while.
Yesterday I was only cold. Today I am
watching the house fill with darkness.
This earth which short years ago was mere earth
has broken up into motionless coils and hoops,
into swiftly moving shades of light and dark.

The bells from the church jangle on.
Dogs are barking. A police car
whoop-whoops three blocks away.
The rasp of these words is a blasphemy
to the Catholic souls of the catechized children.
I want to tell them: *Wait, listen to the whole story!*
But the windy bells are jangling
and for now they are warmed by the Bread inside them
the white, whole, indigestible Bread inside them.

SURVIVORS

When the train stopped at Oymyakon
the temperature was thirty below.
Their feet were stumps of old trees
and their hands those of drowned men.
In some books authors write how suffering is noble.
Do not believe it.
There are miles of tundra empty of meaning
and the sun is not a wafer
in the chalice of northern sky.
The train will go three hundred miles
before it stops again.

In the distance are the coper mines of Dzhezkazgan.
The cars returning are filled only with ore.
But the prisoners ask no questions.
they are not clear and untroubled, these men.
The wind finds each exposed bit of flesh.
The clouded sky, the cold, the tundra
stretching white and empty
is telling them: *Die! Die!*
But they do not answer.
They never answer.

EASTER VIGIL, 1980

Jonquils barely reach green spears
like penance above the snow
and the Holy Saturday streets are softly vague
with the tedious movements of the old
crouching before the marble-like fall
of violet saints touched tonight by benediction.
And I have returned after years to this place
of phantoms and sourceless shadows.

Lilies have vanquished the barren stone
and the calculated violence of crucifixion
has vanished in the midst of Hosannas.
I absolve you, I absolve you
sing the soft buds of the maples
and the birds weave through the timeless
surge of urban isolation.
And I have returned to wonder once again
at the dream of innocence lost here.

Later, walking past the dark windows
of those who winter in Florida, in Tucson
unbowed, untouched by the shadows
I see the old Monseignor.
The red lining of his cape gleams
in the sad lambence of a South Denver streetlamp.
Nice evening, I say as we pass.
Ah yes, some are! he smiles as his cape
glows like wine under the streetlamp.

I walk down to The Shamrock, order a beer and a shot.
And tell no one at the bar any of this
not even the old woman with her rosary
drinking *rose* in a corner booth.

CHILD OF BLUE

--for Melissa

There is a question one woman
never asks of another.
It is respect--queen or peasant--
and seen in the eyes.
Tonight your mother's answer is mine.

My monument of indecision has fallen
to swings, to pebble beaches, to a stage
on which you dance in a clear blue light.
It is your eyes and generations
deep as the sea your mother crossed.

I sailed that sea, a ragged helmsman,
but not adrift, not lost, in the captain's arms
as wave after wave ripped you to land.
I was a beacon half-steady, half-shining.

And land you did exactly like a fish
blue and threshing in the five o'clock light.
No breast dark and peaceful for you, magic lady,
eyes dancing between the spaces of our words,
you chose instead the bright confusion of life.

Bless you, bless your tiny fingers
and blue veins, bless the pain
and the fetal heart monitor,
bless the earth on which you falter for a space
thrashing, freshly caught from the ocean
     to which you'll someday return.
And bless this day which pulled you from the sea
gasping and hungry for life.

SCRIMSHAW

His palms are black with India ink. The nails,
the knuckles, those of a chimney sweep. He takes
whales' teeth and carves them: lighthouses, seagulls,
old sailing ships. His father a Portuguese fisherman
from New Bedford. His father's father and then his
before him. He is like the Navajo in Goldwater's
department store peddling turquoise jewelry. I am
thinking that in a capitalist country, the means of
oppression are subtle. But he is convinced he has
made all the choices which led him here.

He sits in the front window of Woolworth's.
He is the star attraction. Blunt hands which could
pull heavy sienes vibrant with blackfish and flounder,
carving feminine tracery across a chip of ivory.
The skin once tan from ocean sun has lightened in
the store's florescence. I buy a small necklace for
my wife. Promise to write him a poem.

LEARNING ABOUT FREEDOM IN GREENFIELD VILLAGE

I was never far, most of the time,
from Pantano, dust thick on cottonwoods.
Our juniper as good, I said, as your
red cedar. Gambol's oak more delicate
than any shedding acorns into the Mohawk.
Nothing outside was real for me,
nothing uncompared, as we walked
through the woods behind your house: no path,
the way thick with second growth, with gooseberries,
and wild grasses seeding everything that passed:
our shoes, the dog's hair.

The trout stream barely flowed that year.
One shallow pool bled oxygen
like a sugar maple tapped by the awl.
And young trout, pale fingers, swam
clotted, so easy to catch that you moved them
with a small net further upstream, free
to die of common fungus, old age.
But never raccoons, or gills choked by silt.

Yet, where's the sense in that, a grown man?
All life movement toward death anyway.
Still (and we both had work to do
that day), I followed you further into the trees
where the stream foamed over the rocks.
I saw the trout find the place
cool and green and deep. And you were right, Joe.
That was worth something.

SUMMER IN DENVER

Such joyful wounds as August makes
when days are spaces between love,
I reach for the consolation of words
desperate as a bee for the pollen of her touch,
but the sober compromise I make
with fellow bankrupts in bars
brings me further and further from the place
where I knew pain as the only way
of being alive in the world.

Raw honey on pancakes, the morning breeze
through open windows, crickets.
At breakfast, always a flower in her hair
the rich smell of coffee in the air.
These days I seldom eat before noon
and then cereal, cold milk.
Yet the days are still fervid, golden:
the hot indifference of a natural world
that's never been ours.

I walk past the cold spray of August watering
each house blocked out on its little green wedge,
wooden chesspiece on a scrap of felt.
Those in them are secure, as the world spins,
against all minor losses.
But not against death who roams the alleys
nor against boredom who comes to visit
then stays too long.
Only against the desperate compromise with pain
which lets me live are they secure.

Why do you stay here? she asked,
just before she left again for home.
There is ugliness cruising Colfax
in a cocktail dress and high heels;

there is sickness sprawled out behind the Bluebird Bar.
And there is love, I say, racing away,
a faint star in the expanding cosmos
burning, burning beyond anyone's power
to say: Stay!

What does anyone want? Do you know?
    Cobblestone streets in a harbor town,
    white shuttered houses and small gardens,
    fresh fish in the markets, and tall ships in the Bay?
Or warm days in a Tucson barrio with loyal friends
    who later were carried from planes in plastic bags
    or died in Anglo prisons.
I can't go back to where love was
I've got to make it new or go without it.

I am looking for resolution
I am looking for a means to keep the world
from slipping away.
It does, you know. Days like a t.v. re-run,
people one merely tolerates, and passion:
a memory as dim as the yellow photograph
of grandmother as a child.
I live in a city of trampled dreams
trying to find a way to make things new.
I cannot leave until it's done
even as she, to save herself, must run.

Photo: Frenchy Calhoun

MICHAEL HOGAN was born in Newport, Rhode Island in 1943. He is a freelance writer and reviewer, and a consultant on prison literature for the Colorado Humanities Program in Boulder.
He has written six collections of poetry, a book of short stories, and his prose has appeared in numerous anthologies and journals.
Presently he is living in Denver, Colorado.

Hogan works miracles in his poems. His simple words and deep, clear images reaffirm our place on this planet with other living, growing things.

Joseph Bruchac, *The Greenfield Review*

Michael Hogan is an important part of the news from alternative publishing.

Katherine Ames, *Newsweek*

Hogan is a master craftsman with a positive, uplifting humor.
Rochelle Ratner, *Library Journal*